DAVID

A FATHER'S GUIDE TO
BLESSING
HIS CHILDREN

Truth:78

A Father's Guide to Blessing His Children
by David Michael

Published in the United States by Truth78.

All Scripture quotations, unless otherwise noted, are from The Holy Bible,
English Standard Version® (ESV®), copyright © 2001 by Crossway,
a publishing ministry of Good News Publishers. Used by permission.
All rights reserved.

ISBN-13: 978-0-9969870-0-4

Rev. 6.18

Truth:78 / Equipping the Next Generations
to Know, Honor, and Treasure God

Truth78.org · info@Truth78.org · 877.400.1414 · @Truth78org

CONTENTS

BEGINNING A PATTERN OF BLESSING

In the spring of 1991, our daughters were settling into bed after a delightful evening of "family week" activities at our church. We had just watched the film, *The Blessing*,[1] featuring Gary Smalley and John Trent. The film had left me with overwhelming feelings of inadequacy as I pondered my calling, my responsibility, and my deep longing as a father to be a blessing to my children. The weight seemed heavy as our bedtime prayers came to a close.

As a pastor, I was accustomed to pronouncing "benedictions," but not until that moment had I considered pronouncing a benediction or "blessing" over my children. Not until that moment had these girls felt their daddy's right hand on their heads while he called upon the God of Abraham, Isaac, and Jacob to bless them. Not until that moment had I felt such assurance from my Heavenly Father that He would be for my daughters a blessing of infinite value beyond all that I could hope to be. Not until that moment had I, with such earnest and desperate desire, looked into the eyes of each daughter and said,

> **May the <u>LORD</u> bless you and keep you!**
> **May the <u>LORD</u> make His face shine upon you**
> **and be gracious to you!**

---

1. *The Blessing*, a 60-minute videocassette produced by Jeff Bowden. (Nashville, Tenn.: Thomas Nelson, 1991).

May the **LORD** lift up His countenance upon you and give you peace!

That night "the blessing" was added to the bedtime routine. As our daughters made their way toward womanhood, our routine changed. The after-supper wrestling matches, bedtime stories on my lap, and airplane rides into bed became either impossible or no longer "cool," but for both daddy and daughters the daily bedtime blessing continued to be cherished (and "cool") as long as they were living at home.

Many bedtimes have come and gone since that first night of blessing in the spring of 1991. Today, the two little girls are women, and the bedtime routine we once knew is now a precious memory. Along the way, there have been poignant moments of blessing that even now, as I call them to mind, bring a lump to my throat and tears to my eyes. Moments in dorm rooms and airports where we embraced and prayed one last prayer and one last blessing before the miles separated us. Moments at graduations, baptisms, and other significant events when I would look into the eyes of my grown-up "little girls." With my hand on their shoulders and familiar words of blessing on their heads, my heart overflowed again and again with familiar longings that the Father of infinite blessing would satisfy them beyond all that their earthly father could hope for.

Today I can look into the eyes of two more little girls and one little boy (our grandchildren), and what I see is not only the eyes of their mother; I see the eyes of the next generation. The longing in this grandpa's heart is the same as the longing in the heart of this father for more than three decades—the longing that "One generation shall commend [God's] works to another, and shall declare [God's] mighty acts" (Psalm 145:4).

WHAT IS
A BLESSING?

Several months after I began regularly blessing my daughters, I was introduced to Rolf Garborg's book, *The Family Blessing*.[1] Garborg not only gave me a biblical foundation for what I was discovering about the blessing, but he also inspired me with the experience and testimony of a man who had been blessing his children for more than 18 years. I urge aspiring "blessers" to read Garborg's book for a much more thorough treatment of the subject than I will be able to provide in this guide.

Garborg identifies four different categories of blessings in Scripture, one of which is "the blessing spoken by one person to another, often in the name of God."[2] Garborg goes on to explain that within this category there is a general use of the word that simply means "to speak well of, to express praise."[3] There is also a more specific use that defines blessing as "the intentional act of speaking God's favor and power into someone's life, often accompanied by a symbolic gesture such as laying hands on the person."[4] This specific use of the word is what I have in mind as I encourage blessing in the church, and especially in Christian homes where it can become another significant way to nurture the faith of our children and bestow God's blessing on their lives.

---

1. Garborg, Rolf. *The Family Blessing*. (Dallas: Word Publishing Company, 1990).
2. Ibid, 12.
3. Ibid, 13
4. Ibid, 13.

BIBLICAL UNDERSTANDING OF BLESSING

Although a blessing could be considered a form of prayer, there is a distinction between the two. Simply put, in prayer we direct our attention toward God. We "ask God for things,"[1] which may include His "blessing." A blessing, on the other hand, comes from God and is directed toward His people. When we bless, we are invoking, summoning, or calling upon God's blessing for the benefit of another. When we bless, we seek God's blessing to flow through us to another.

We see this clearly in Numbers 6:22-27 when the LORD, through Moses, gives this instruction to Aaron and his sons: "'Thus you shall bless the people of Israel: you shall say to them, The LORD bless you, and keep you; the LORD make his face to shine upon you and be gracious to you; the LORD lift up his countenance upon you and give you peace. So *shall they put my name upon* the people of Israel, and I will bless them.'" (Emphasis added.)

Notice how many times the LORD's name is identified with the blessing that Aaron and his sons were to bestow upon the

---

1. For further discussion of this understanding of prayer, see John Piper's sermon on Colossians 4:2-4, "Devote Yourselves to Prayer," January 9, 2000, available at desiringGod.org.

people of Israel. It is the LORD who blesses and keeps and makes His face shine on His people. It is the LORD who directs His countenance and smile toward us, and gives His grace and peace to all.

In verse 27, we can see clearly that the sons of Aaron were given authority by God to call for His blessing upon an individual or group: "So shall they put my name upon the people of Israel, and I will bless them." This is not unlike the authority Jesus gave His disciples. In John 20:23, He tells them, "If you forgive the sins of any, they are forgiven them; if you withhold forgiveness from any, it is withheld." In Luke 9:1, He calls His 12 disciples and gives them power and authority over all the demons, as well as to heal diseases. And in Acts 3:6, Peter declares to the lame man, "I have no silver and gold, but what I do have I give to you. In the name of Jesus Christ of Nazareth, rise up and walk!"

It appears that blessings were a regular part of Israel's experience at home and when they gathered as a people. As Laban was parting company with Jacob and his family, he "arose and kissed his grandchildren and his daughters and blessed them" (Genesis 31:55). Jacob, at the end of his life, gathered his children together and "blessed them, blessing each with the blessing suitable to him" (Genesis 49:28). Aaron "lifted up his hands toward the people and blessed [Israel], and he came down from offering the sin offering and the burnt offering and the peace offerings" (Leviticus 9:22). After Joshua had given the half-tribe of Manasseh its possession, he "blessed them and sent them away" (Joshua 22:6). King David brought the ark of God back to Jerusalem and "blessed the people in the name of the LORD of hosts" and then "returned to bless his household" (2 Samuel 6:18-20).

Twice in the Gospels, Jesus blesses people. In Mark 10, we are told that He took the children into His arms "and blessed them, laying his hands on them" (Mark 10:15). And just before ascending to heaven, Luke tells us that Jesus led His disciples "out as far as Bethany, and lifting up his hands he blessed them. While he blessed them, he parted from them and was carried up into heaven. And they worshiped Him and returned to Jerusalem with great joy" (Luke 24:50-52).

One of the more notable blessings in the Bible was the blessing Isaac intended for Esau, but gave instead to Jacob when Jacob deceived him. This blessing had prophetic qualities that are unique. This blessing was not something the sons of Isaac had received before. It came when Isaac knew his days on earth were ending (Genesis 27:2-4), and when he was ready to pass on the authority and the covenant blessing that had been handed down to him by his father Abraham. Once pronounced, it was irrevocable. Even when Isaac realized he had been tricked, it was impossible for him to remove the blessing from Jacob (Genesis 27:33-40).

We see the prophetic blessing again at the end of Jacob's life when Joseph's sons are blessed. Joseph's unsuccessful attempt to move Jacob's right hand of blessing from Ephraim to Manasseh points to the prophetic significance. Not only are the words of blessing important, but so is the placement of the hand (Genesis 48:9-20).

Such prophetic blessings were extraordinary and mainly associated with God's covenant purposes as they were revealed from one generation to the next. The kind of blessing that we do in the context of home and family does not carry this same prophetic weight. When I place my hand on my daughter's head and say "May you be blessed as a woman who fears the LORD, a woman who finds great delight in the LORD's commands," I am seeking God's favor upon her in the hope that she will be a woman who fears the LORD, but I am not declaring in a prophetic sense that she will become such a woman.

RESPONSIBILITY AND AUTHORITY TO BLESS

We saw in Numbers 6 that instructions concerning the blessing were directed specifically to the Levitical priesthood. This responsibility was reaffirmed in Deuteronomy 10:8 following the death of Aaron when "the LORD set apart the tribe of Levi to carry the ark of the covenant of the LORD to stand before the LORD to minister to him and *to bless in his name, to this day,*" and again in Deuteronomy 21:5 when Moses said to Israel "...the LORD your God has chosen [the sons of Levi] to minister to him *and to bless in the name of the LORD.*" (Emphasis added.)

Although there are no comparable instructions to fathers, it is clear that the responsibility and authority to bless carried over into family life. It was usually the father who assumed the responsibility for blessing his children.

From the biblical teaching and the examples we have observed, it seems reasonable that spiritual leaders in the home and church are free to and should be encouraged to pronounce blessings. Furthermore, if we consider the "priesthood" of all believers (1 Peter 2:5) and the general

> **Spiritual leaders in the home and the church should be encouraged to bless those they are called to lead.**
>
> **—DAVID MICHAEL**

instructions given by Jesus and Paul (Luke 6:28; Romans 12:14), it seems that under the New Covenant any believer should feel the freedom to bless others in this way.

Spiritual leaders in the home and the church should be encouraged to bless those they are called to lead. I believe the church is well-served when pastors, elders, small group leaders, ministry leaders, and Sunday school teachers bless those they are called to serve and lead. Similarly, I have witnessed the benefit to families and marriages when husbands and fathers make the effort to bless their wives and children. This resource has come from a desire that my brothers in Christ would join me in the practice of blessing, and then enjoy the fruits of blessing described in the next chapter.

THE FRUITS
OF BLESSING

In the years that I have been using blessings in my role as a father, grandfather, and pastor, I have discovered, through my own experience and the experience of others, that alongside the joy of being an instrument of blessing in another's life, there are many fruits to enjoy from this practice. Here is a "taste" of what has come:

1. The opportunity to acknowledge God as the source of every blessing.

Based on the biblical understanding of blessing, the most obvious benefit is that it is a means of God blessing His people. Even though there is a difference between a prayer and a blessing, God's response to a blessing is similar to His response to our prayers. The LORD delights in magnifying His name by fulfilling the desires of those who fear Him (Psalm 145:19).

He is not obligated to act according to the blessings we invoke any more than He is obligated to give us what we ask for in prayer. Nevertheless, we bless in the same confidence that we pray, knowing that God is faithful to His Word and delights to act in response to the faith of His people.

2. Blessings touch the future.

Blessings have a forward view. This is obvious in the prophetic blessings of the patriarchs, but it is also true of ordinary blessings. The fact that many blessings were given at moments of parting or separation points to the future orientation of the blessing. When we say to someone, "The LORD bless you and keep you," we are not only seeking God's blessing for the moment, but desire God's blessing to continue as they go. We commend them to the "LORD, who made heaven and earth" with confidence that He will be their "keeper" and not let their "foot be moved," and that He will keep their "going out" and their "coming in from this time forth and forevermore" (Psalm 121).

As years were added to my daughters' lives, there were fewer and fewer opportunities to personally watch over them. Hours of physical separation from them have become months. One day I will be completely removed from their lives. As they were growing up, I was keenly aware of how quickly time was passing, and with it my fleeting influence upon them. For me, the blessing was an opportunity to touch their lives for the present, and for the inevitable day when time and miles, and death will separate us.

As I face these separations, I am encouraged by the biblical image of the Lord storing up the prayers of His people and responding to them on His timetable. One place I see this is in Acts 10:4, when the Lord spoke to Cornelius and said, "Your prayers and your alms have ascended as a memorial before God." At the right moment, God answered those prayers and granted this Gentile the repentance that leads to life.

Another place I see this is in Exodus 3:9 when the LORD spoke to Moses and said, "the cry of the people of Israel has come to me, and I have also seen the oppression with which the Egyptians oppress them." These cries had been ascending to the LORD for more than 400 years. When the time was right, He poured out the fruit of those prayers.

As I bless my children in the presence of God, I am conscious that God hears and remembers the blessing. He remembers today's blessing on my children, and He will remember it 45 years from now, when the time is right, and pour out His favor on my octogenarian daughters in response to their daddy's blessing decades before.

I will take this idea one step further and say that even beyond the lives of my children I expect there to be fruit from these blessings. So many of the blessings that I give my children reflect my desire that the fruit of God's work through me will continue to every generation coming after me until Jesus returns. Some of these blessings include: "May He watch over your coming and going, both now and forever" (Psalm 121:8); "May your name be remembered forever" (Psalm 112:6); "May you dwell in the house of the LORD forever" (Psalm 23:6); "Even to the next generation may you and your children be blessed" (adapted from Psalm 112:2); and "May the LORD give you pleasure at His right hand, forever" (adapted from Psalm 16:11).

Since I first began blessing my daughters, I have had a vision of a night, 150 years from now. I imagine a young man kneeling beside his child's bed, pronouncing the same blessing that his Great Great Great Grandfather Michael pronounced over his great great grandmother. This is more than a sentimental desire. It is rooted in an earnest prayer that a river of faith will flow through my descendants, and that all of them will fear the LORD (Psalm 103:17).

> **As I bless my children in the presence of God, I am conscious that God hears and remembers... today's blessing on my children, and He will remember it 45 years from now, when the time is right...**
>
> **—DAVID MICHAEL**

3. The blessing gives my children a vision for what I desire most for them.

The blessing is not only given in the presence of God, but also in the presence of the ones being blessed. As parents, we care that our children have a good education, good health, a good spouse, and a good job. We expend a great deal of energy and resources toward these ends. As important as these things are, they fade when compared to those things that have eternal value. The blessing is a way for my children to hear and understand what their daddy desires most for them. Night after night, they hear me express my desire that they fear the LORD and delight to do His will. They hear the hope that the LORD will be their counselor all the days of their lives, and that they will always set the LORD before them. They catch a vision for being like Mount Zion, which cannot be shaken but endures forever (Psalm 125:1), and for having their names be remembered by the LORD forever (Psalm 112:6).

4. The blessing can be a means of comfort and reassurance.

The blessing is a reminder of the presence of God and His care for us: "Even while you sleep, may the LORD instruct your heart" (adapted from Psalm 16:7), "May the LORD watch over you and be a shade at your right hand so the sun will not harm you by day nor the moon by night" (adapted from Psalm 121:5-6), and "May the LORD answer you when you pray and relieve you in distress" (adapted from Psalm 4:1).

I have heard several testimonies from parents whose children had different problems related to fear at night. In many of these cases, there was a remarkable change after the parent began blessing the child at bedtime. As a pastor, I regularly bless people I visit in the hospital because I have found that speaking God's Word over a person in this way can bring the LORD's peace to anxious souls awaiting surgery or struggling with a critical illness or disease. For those who grieve, the blessing brings hope and comfort as we call upon the God of hope to fill them with all joy and peace, as they trust in Him that they may abound in hope through the power of the Holy Spirit (Romans 15:13).

5. The blessing can help heal strained relationships.

The blessing can give children assurance of parental love after a hard day. It is not uncommon for there to be days when a parent and child become irritated or angry with each other and perhaps say or do things that are hurtful. There are also days when a child disobeys and is punished by the same hand that blesses. At the end of such a day, it can be a great encouragement for that child to hear words of blessing directed toward him. It provides a way for the parent to say, "In spite of what has happened between us today, I still love you, and the desire of my heart is for your good."

The blessing can have this effect on adults as well. It is disarming when a blessing is pronounced on someone in a relationship that is strained. It is very difficult to stay angry with a person who is sincerely blessing you. The defenses will often drop while the doors of forgiveness and reconciliation open.

6. The blessing can help strengthen the bonds of affection between children and parents.

In what seemed like a blink of the eye, Sally and I were "empty-nesters" walking past two empty bedrooms at night. The joy of tucking my girls into bed with a prayer and a blessing is now only a precious memory. As adults, I hope my daughters can forget my shortcomings and the mistakes I made along the way with my careless words and foolish actions. As they look back over the years when they were young, I pray they will never forget the heart of a daddy who desired more than anything that they be filled with God and enjoy Him forever.

I believe the blessings have helped my daughters to see this desire in me. God has used the blessings to knit our hearts together with a deep affection and love, which I trust will endure for a lifetime. By itself, the blessing cannot take the place of faithful parenting. We ought not be deceived into thinking that we can bless our children once a day while ignoring them and their needs the rest of the time. However, combined with faithful parenting, the blessing can be a powerful tool in strengthening the bonds of affection and establishing our children firmly in faith.

7. The practice of blessing encourages men in their roles as spiritual leaders.

In the previous chapter, "Responsibility and Authority to Bless," I encouraged husbands and fathers to initiate the practice of blessing in their homes and gave reasons why I believe the church and the home would both benefit. Little more needs to be said here except to emphasize that when a man is regularly blessing his wife and children, he is more likely to give spiritual leadership in other areas of personal and family life.

BLESSING SUGGESTIONS

1. Two things that I find important in blessing someone are eye contact and touch. I make every effort to look the people in the eye when I am blessing them. I use my eyes to communicate as much sincerity and love as I possibly can. Placing a hand on a person's shoulder, head, or back is not only a way to communicate the affection that is often associated with the blessing, but it is also symbolic of "imparting" or "invoking" a blessing of God upon them. This same idea is communicated in group settings by lifting one or both hands over the group as the blessing is pronounced.

2. I encourage people to memorize the blessings because it frees us to make eye contact with the people we are blessing, and it helps the words of blessing flow from the heart. Memorizing can be almost effortless if you are blessing someone daily.

3. Some of the blessings in this collection are direct quotes from a portion of Scripture. Others were inspired by a text and adapted to fit a blessing format. Almost all of these blessings are the fruit of personal Bible reading and prayer when I was gripped by a specific truth or the promise and then turned it into a blessing. As you meditate on God's Word, you will undoubtedly see things that will inspire you to pray for others. As God speaks to you through His Word consider turning His Word into a blessing, and watch God minister His blessing through you.

07

ONE FINAL
THOUGHT

I began this booklet by describing a point in time when I felt a desperate need to be a blessing to my children and how the practice of blessing grew out of that need. Today I feel less desperate, but more responsible than ever in the calling that is on my life to be a means of blessing to my children, my wife, and the brothers and sisters I am serving as a pastor. Regularly pronouncing blessings has given me a daily reminder that God is ultimately the One who will see to it that my loved ones are blessed, which is what helps minimize the desperation I feel.

Blessings remind me that I can be an instrument of blessing, not only with a particular set of words and the laying on of a hand, but by the way I live my life and demonstrate my faith before those who are looking to me as an example. As you begin or continue in blessing others, I want to leave you with one of my favorite blessings that reflects my earnest prayer and desire that God use you to bless others with your words and with your life.

May you bless others as a person
who fears the LORD, and who greatly
delights in His commandments.
May your children be mighty
in the land.
Even to the next generation,
may you and your children be blessed.
May you find your wealth
and your riches in God.
May your righteousness endure forever.
Even in the darkness
may the light dawn for you.
May you abound in love, joy, peace,
patience, kindness, goodness,
faithfulness, gentleness,
and self-control.
May you never be shaken.
And may your name, and the names
of all whom you bless, be remembered
by the LORD, forever. Amen!

—PSALM 112:1-6 AND GALATIANS 5:22-23

BLESSINGS

Genesis 48:15-16 (Jacob's Blessing)

May the God before whom Abraham and Isaac walked,
the God who has been my shepherd all my life, to this day,
and who has redeemed me from all evil—
bless you and let His name live on in you
and in your children after you, forever. Amen!

Numbers 6:24-26 (Aaron's Blessing)

May the LORD bless you and keep you.
May the LORD make His face shine upon you
and be gracious to you.
May the LORD lift up His countenance upon you
and give you peace. Amen!

1 Kings 8:57-60

May the LORD our God be with you as He has been with me.
May He never leave you or forsake you.
May He incline your heart toward Him
and cause you to walk in all His ways.
Day and night may your prayers be near to Him.
May the LORD maintain your cause and the cause of all His people
so that you and all the peoples of the earth may know
that the LORD is God, and there is none other! Amen!

Psalm 1

May the LORD bless you and give you
the courage not to walk in the counsel of the wicked;
the faith not to stand in the way of sinners;
and the resolve not to sit in the seat of scoffers.
May your delight be in the law of the LORD
that you might meditate on it day and night.
May you be like a tree planted by streams of water,
that yields its fruit in season
and its leaf does not wither.
May the LORD prosper all that you do for His glory,
and watch over your way
so that you will stand in the judgment
and join the congregation of the righteous forever. Amen!

Psalm 4

May the LORD be gracious to you
and give you relief in distress.
May the LORD establish you as a godly [man or woman]
who trusts in Him.
May He lift up the light of His face upon you
and put gladness in your heart that exceeds all earthly joy.
May the LORD make you dwell in safety.
so that when you lie down,
you may you sleep in peace. Amen!

Psalm 13:5-6

May the LORD deal bountifully with you all the days of your life,
And may you always
trust in the steadfast, love of the LORD,
rejoice in His salvation, and sing His praises
forever and ever. Amen!

Psalm 16:7-11

May the LORD be your counselor all the days of your life.
Even in the night, may the LORD instruct your heart.
May you always set the LORD before you.
And may He always be at your right hand
*   so that you shall never be shaken.*
May your heart be glad, your tongue rejoice,
*   and your body dwell secure.*
May the LORD make known to you the path of life,
*   fill you with joy in His presence,*
*   and give you pleasures at His right hand forever. Amen!*

Psalm 23

May the LORD be your shepherd,
*   and bless you with all that you need.*
May He make you lie down in green pastures,
*   and lead you beside still waters, and restore your soul.*
May He lead you in paths of righteousness
*   for His name's sake.*
May His rod and staff comfort you
*   so that you fear no evil*
*   even when you walk through the valley of the shadow of death.*
May the LORD prepare a table before you
*   in the presence of your enemies.*
May He anoint your head with oil.
May your cup of joy overflow.
May the LORD's goodness and mercy
*   follow you all the days of your life.*
And may you dwell in the house of the LORD forever. Amen!

Psalm 46:1-7

May the LORD be your refuge and strength.
  and a very present help in trouble.
May He keep you from fear even though the earth gives way,
  or the mountains be moved into the heart of the sea,
  or the waters roar and foam,
  or the mountains tremble at its swelling.
May the LORD lead you to the river
  whose streams make glad the city of God,
  the holy habitation of the Most High.
May the LORD of hosts be with you;
and the God of Jacob be your fortress forever. Amen!

Psalm 67

May the LORD bless you
  so that His way may be known on the earth.
May the LORD be gracious to you
  so that all the earth may know the saving power of His way.
And may the LORD make His face to shine upon you
  so that the nations will be glad and sing for joy
  and praise His name to all generations. Amen!

Psalm 91

May you dwell in the shelter of the Most High
  and abide in the shadow of the Almighty.
May the LORD be your refuge, your fortress,
  and the God in whom you trust.
May the LORD command His angels concerning you
  to guard you in all your ways.
May He answer you when you call and be with you in trouble.
May the LORD rescue and honor you.
With long life may He satisfy you and show you His salvation.
Amen!

Psalm 103:1-5

May your soul bless the LORD all the days of your life.
With all that is within you, may you bless His holy name.
May you never forget the benefits of Him who
    forgives all your sins,
    heals all your diseases,
    and redeems your life from the pit.
May the LORD satisfy your years with good things
    and crown your life with His steadfast love
    and tender mercies forever. Amen!

Psalm 112:1-6; Galatians 5:22-23

May you be a [man or woman] *who fears the LORD*
    and greatly delights in His commandments.
May your children be mighty in the land.
Even to the next generation,
    may you and your children be blessed.
May you find your wealth and your riches in God.
May your righteousness endure forever.
Even in the darkness may the light dawn for you.
May you abound in love, joy, peace, patience, kindness,
    goodness, faithfulness, gentleness, and self-control.
May you never be shaken.
And may your name, [full name],
    be remembered by the LORD, forever. Amen!

Psalm 119 (selected portions)

May the LORD deal bountifully with you [17]
and open your eyes to see wonderful things from His Word. [18]
May His Word be a lamp to your feet
and a light to your path. [105]
May you treasure His Word in your heart
so that you will not sin against Him. [11]
May you observe the testimonies of the LORD
and delight in His way more than in riches. [14]
May the LORD give you the understanding to keep His commands
and observe them with your whole heart. [34]
May the LORD give you life according to His steadfast love [159]
and hope in His salvation forever. [166] *Amen!*

Psalm 121:5-8

May the LORD be your keeper.
May He be a shade on your right hand
so that the sun will not strike you by day
nor the moon by night.
May the LORD keep you from all evil and watch over your life.
May He keep your going out and your coming in,
from this time forth and forevermore. Amen!

Psalm 125:1-2

May you trust the LORD with all your heart.
May you be like Mount Zion, which cannot be moved,
but abides forever.
As the mountains surround Jerusalem,
may the LORD surround you from this time forth
and forevermore. Amen!

Romans 15:13

May the God of hope fill you with all joy and peace in believing,
*   so that by the power of the Holy Spirit,*
*   you may abound in hope. Amen!*

2 Corinthians 13:14

May the grace of the Lord Jesus Christ, and the love of God,
*   and the fellowship of the Holy Spirit be with you*
*   from this time forth and forevermore. Amen!*

Ephesians 3:14-19

And now, may our great and eternal Father bless you.
May He strengthen your inner being
*   with His power through His Spirit.*
May Christ dwell in your heart through faith.
May you be rooted and grounded in love.
May you have the strength to comprehend with all the saints
*   what is the breadth and length and height and depth,*
*   and to know the love of Christ that surpasses knowledge.*
May you be filled with all the fullness of God
*   according to the riches of His grace.*
And may you exalt His glorious name forever and ever. Amen!

Ephesians 3:20-21

Unto Him who is able to do far more abundantly
*   than all we ask or think,*
*   according to the power at work within us,* [and beside us,
    and above us, and beneath us, and all around us,]
To Him be the glory
    [in your life,] *in the church, and in Christ Jesus,*
*   to all generations forever and ever. Amen!*

Ephesians 6:10-17

May you be a [man or woman] *who is strong in the Lord
    and in the strength of His might.
May you be blessed with the whole armor of God
    so that you can stand against the schemes of the devil.
May you stand firm
    with the belt of truth buckled around your waist,
    and the breastplate of righteousness in place,
    and your feet fitted with the readiness of the Gospel of peace.
May you take up the shield of faith,
    the helmet of salvation,
    and the sword of the Spirit, which is the Word of God,
    so that you may be able to stand in the evil day
    and boldly proclaim the mystery of the Gospel. Amen!*

Colossians 1:9-12

*May you be filled with the knowledge of God's will
    in all spiritual wisdom and understanding,
    so as to walk in a manner worthy of the Lord
    fully pleasing to Him in all respects.
May you bear fruit in every good work
    and increase in the knowledge of God.
May the Lord strengthen you with all power,
    according to His glorious might,
    for all endurance and patience with joy.
And may you give thanks to the Father,
    who qualifies us to share in the inheritance of the saints
    in light, forever. Amen!*

1 Thessalonians 5:23-24

May the God of peace Himself sanctify you completely.
May your whole spirit, soul, and body be kept blameless
    at the coming of our Lord Jesus Christ.
And may you always trust the faithful One who calls you
    and will surely accomplish your redemption. Amen!

2 Thessalonians 1:11-12

To this end, I bless you in the name of the Lord,
    that the Lord may make you worthy of His calling
    and fulfill every resolve for good
    and every work of faith, by His power.
May the name of our Lord Jesus be glorified in you
    and you in Him,
    according to the grace of our God
    and our Lord Jesus Christ,
    to whom be glory forever. Amen!

2 Thessalonians 2:16-17; 3:16

May the Lord Jesus Christ Himself and God our Father,
    who loves us
    and gave us eternal comfort and good hope through grace,
    comfort and establish your heart in every good work and word.
May the Lord of peace Himself give you peace
    at all times in every way.
And may the grace of the Lord Jesus Christ
    be with you now and forever. Amen!

Hebrews 12:1

May the LORD bless you like the mighty men and women of faith
who have gone before you.
May He give you the grace to lay aside every weight and sin,
which so easily entangles us.
May He give you the endurance to run the race that is set
before you, and give you eyes that look to Jesus,
as the founder and perfecter of our faith,
and may He set before you the joy
that enabled Christ to endure the cross,
despise the shame
until He was seated at the right hand of God forever. Amen!

Hebrews 13:20-21

May the God of Peace
who brought again from the dead our Lord Jesus,
the great shepherd of the sheep
by the blood of the eternal covenant
equip you with everything good to do His will,
and work in you that which is pleasing in His sight
through Jesus Christ,
to whom be glory forever and ever. Amen!

1 Peter 1:3-9

May the God and Father of our Lord Jesus Christ
cause you to be born again to a living hope,
and to an inheritance that is imperishable, undefiled,
unfading, and kept in heaven for you.
May the Lord guard you through faith
for a salvation that is ready to be revealed.
And may the outcome of your faith, even when tested by fire,
result in praise, glory, and honor at the revelation of Jesus Christ,
For His glory, forever and ever. Amen!

Grace

*May there be grace to you from God our Father
      and the Lord Jesus Christ.* (EPHESIANS 1:2)
May you be saved through His grace. (ACTS 15:11)
May you grow in His grace. (2 PETER 3:18)
May you be strengthened by His grace. (2 TIMOTHY 2:1)
May you continue in His grace. (ACTS 13:43)
May you draw near with confidence to His throne of grace.
      (HEBREWS 4:16)
May He forgive your sins according to the riches of His grace.
      (EPHESIANS 1:7)
May you bear witness to His Word of grace. (ACTS 14:3)
May you set your hope fully on His grace. (1 PETER 1:13)
To the praise of His glorious grace. (EPHESIANS 1:6)
Both now and to the day of eternity. (2 PETER 3:18) *Amen!*

A FATHER'S BLESSING APP

A Father's Blessing App will help you establish and sustain a regular pattern for blessing your children (and others) that will encourage and strengthen their faith. The app conveniently includes the blessings from this booklet and allows you to create your own blessings and keep them so you can easily pronounce blessings at home or on the go.

Learn more and download the app from iTunes for iOS or Google Play for Android.

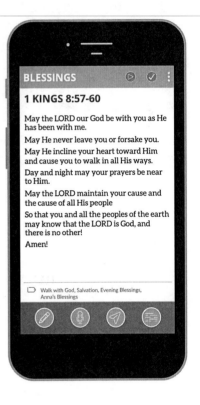

A Father's Blessing App Features

- The text from this booklet: *A Father's Guide to Blessing His Children*
- The 29 Truth78 blessings included in this booklet
- Option to add new blessings (import Scripture from any translation and customize to create your own blessings)
- Ability to modify/personalize existing and new blessings
- Tags for organizing blessings (by person, occasion, etc.)
- Ability to send recorded or written blessing via text or email
- Two quizzes—Quick Blanks and Recite Aloud—to help you memorize the blessing
- System for marking blessings when they are memorized

ABOUT TRUTH78

Truth78 is a vision-oriented ministry for the next generations. Our vision is that the next generations know, honor, and treasure God, setting their hope in Christ alone, so that they will live as faithful disciples for the glory of God.

Our mission is to nurture the faith of the next generations by equipping the church and home with resources and training that instruct the mind, engage the heart, and influence the will through proclaiming the whole counsel of God.

Values that undergird the development of our resources and training are that they be God-centered, Bible-saturated, Gospel-focused, Christ-exalting, Spirit-dependent, doctrinally grounded, and discipleship-oriented.

Resources for Church and Home

Truth78 currently offers the following categories of resources and training materials for equipping the church and home:

Vision-Casting and Training

We offer a wide variety of booklets, video and audio seminars, articles, and other practical training resources that highlight and further expound our vision, mission, and values, as well as our educational philosophy and methodology. Many of these resources are freely distributed through our website. These resources and training serve to assist ministry leaders, volunteers, and parents in implementing Truth78's vision and mission in their churches and homes.

Curriculum

We publish materials designed for formal Bible instruction. The scope and sequence of these materials reflects our commitment to teach children and youth the whole counsel of God over the course of their education. Materials include curricula for Sunday school, Midweek Bible programs, Backyard Bible Clubs or Vacation Bible School, and Intergenerational studies. Most of these materials can be adapted for use in Christian schools and education in the home.

Parenting and Family Discipleship

We have produced a variety of materials and training resources designed to help parents in their role in discipling their children. These include booklets, video presentations, family devotionals, children's books, articles, and other recommended resources. Furthermore, our curricula include Growing in Faith Together (GIFT) Pages to help parents apply what is taught in the classroom to their child's daily experience in order to nurture faith.

Bible Memory

Our Fighter Verses Bible memory program is designed to encourage churches, families, and individuals in the lifelong practice and love of Bible memory. The Fighter Verses program utilizes an easy-to-use Bible memory system with carefully chosen verses to help fight the fight of faith. It is available in print, on FighterVerses.com, and as an app for smart phones and other mobile devices. The Fighter Verses App includes review reminders, quizzes, songs, a devotional, and other memory helps. For pre-readers, Foundation Verses uses simple images to help young children memorize 76 key verses. We also offer a study, devotional guide, and coloring book that correspond to Set 1 of the Fighter Verses. Visit FighterVerses.com for the weekly devotional blog and for free memory aids.

For more information on any of these resources contact:

Truth78.org
info@Truth78.org
877.400.1414
@Truth78org